SELF AND SELF-MANAGEMENT

ESSAYS ABOUT EXISTING

BY

ARNOLD BENNETT

Copyright © 2019 Read Books Ltd.
This book is copyright and may not be
reproduced or copied in any way without
the express permission of the publisher in writing

British Library Cataloguing-in-Publication Data
A catalogue record for this book is available from
the British Library

ON HAPPINESS.

Lives there a man within this vale of tears
However long he may have traversed life,
That e'er possessed a state of real bliss?
Experience wisely teacheth all mankind,
Whilst passing through this sublunary scene,
That all must share distress—and care—and woe.
Man enters life buoyed up with flattering Hope
Which strews sweet flowers along the rugged path
Of life's, oft checkered, varied pilgrimage,
Tempting the traveller still to journey on,
Pursuing as he goes some darling scheme
Foster'd by Hope within the heart's recess.
   Talent diversified adorns mankind,—
And various characters must be combined
To play Life's drama on the world's wide stage;
Each hath a part assigned him here to act:
Widely their aims may differ, and their views
May vary as the colours in the bow
That arches the ethereal vault of heaven;
Yet all dissention to one focus points:—
That phantom Happiness, each breast pursues!
O! seek her not amid tumultuous scenes!—

Midst busy life!—she seldom loves to dwell
Among the great—in cities, or in courts—
But more retiringly disposed, she seeks
The calmer haunts of men in humbler ranks.
But wheresoe'er she roams, in sylvan scenes,
O'er hills, through dales, or in the grove's recess,
Or on the verdant plain, she still eludes
The eager grasp of disappointed man!

   Depend not on a dire deceitful world,—
But point affection to a higher sphere;
And boast a conscience void of all offence
Towards thy Creator and thy fellow-man.
Whatever part here called upon to act,
Use all exertion to perform it well;—
Yet be not too ambitious of applause:
'Tis but a chosen few the audience clap;
And when the curtain drops,—and man hath played
His arduous part, he then retiring falls
Behind the scenes. There, Life's garb thrown off,
Is his performance judged.—If acted right,
'Tis then is met a just reward for all,—
He has applause from the celestial band,
And gains what he has vainly sought below,
True Happiness!—this,—heaven alone bestows.

                              - ELIZABETH BIGLEY CHADWICK

CONTENTS

	PAGE
RUNNING AWAY FROM LIFE	3
SOME AXIOMS ABOUT WAR-WORK	25
THE DIARY HABIT	45
A DANGEROUS LECTURE TO A YOUNG WOMAN	65
THE COMPLETE FUSSER	85
THE MEANING OF FROCKS	103

RUNNING AWAY FROM LIFE

RUNNING AWAY FROM LIFE

1

I WILL take the extreme case of the social butterfly, because it has the great advantage of simplicity. This favourite variety of the lepidopteral insects is always spoken of as female. But as the variety persists from generation to generation obviously it cannot be of one sex only. And, as a fact, there are indubitably male social butterflies, though the differences between the male and the female may be slight. I shall, however, confine myself to the case of the female social butterfly—again for the sake of simplicity.

This beautiful creature combines the habits of the butterfly with the habits of the moth. For whereas the moth flies only by night and the butterfly flies only by day, the social butterfly flies both by day and by night. She is universally despised and condemned, and almost universally envied : one of the strangest among the many strange facts of natural history. She lives with a single purpose—to be for ever in the movement—not any particular movement, but *the* movement, which is a grand combined tendency comprising all lesser tendencies. For the social butterfly the constituents of the movement are chiefly men, theatres, restaurants, dances, noise, and hurry. The minor constituents may and do frequently change, but the major constituents have not changed for a considerable number of years. The minor constituents of the movement are usually ' serious,' and hence in a minor way the social butterfly is serious. If books happen to be of the movement, she will learn the names of books and authors, and in urgent crises will even read. If music, she will learn to distinguish from all other sounds the sounds which are of the movement, the sounds at which she must shut her eyes in ecstasy and sigh. If social reform, she will at once be ready to reform everybody and everything except herself and her existence. If charity or mercifulness, she will be charitable or merciful according to the latest devices and in the latest frocks. Yes, and if war happens to be of the movement, she will be serious about the war.

You observe how sarcastic I am about the social butterfly. It is necessary to be so. The social butterfly never has since the earliest times been mentioned in print without sarcasm or pity, and she never will be. She is greatly to be pitied. What is her aim? Her aim, like the aim of most people except the very poor (whose aim is simply to keep alive), is happiness. But the unfortunate creature, as you and I can so clearly see, has confused happiness with pleasure. She runs day and night after pleasure—that is to say, after distraction : eating, drinking, posing, seeing, being seen, laughing, jostling, and the singular delight of continual imitation. She is only alive in public, and the whole of her days and nights are spent in being in public, or in preparing to be in public, or in recovering from the effects of being in public. Habit drives her on from one excitement to another. She flies eternally from something mysterious and sinister which is eternally overtaking her. You and I know that she is never happy—she is only intoxicated or narcotised by a drug that she calls pleasure. And her youth is going ; her figure is going ; her complexion is practically gone. She is laying up naught for the future save disappointment, dissatisfaction, disillusion, and no doubt rheumatism. And all this inordinate, incredible folly springs from a wrong and childish interpretation of the true significance of happiness.

II

How much wiser, you say, and indeed we all say, is that other young woman who has chosen the part of content. She has come to terms with the universe. She is not for ever gadding about in search of something which she has not got, and which not one person in a hundred round about her has got. She has said : ' The universe is stronger than I am. I will accommodate myself to the universe.'

And she acts accordingly. She makes the best of her lot. She treats her body in a sane manner, and she treats her mind in a sane manner. She has perceived the futility of what is known as pleasure in circles where they play bridge and organise charity fêtes on the Field of the Cloth of Gold. She has frankly admitted that youth is fleeting, and that part of it must be spent in making preparations against the rigours of old age. She seeks her pleasure in literature and the arts because such pleasure strengthens instead of weakening the mind, and never palls. She is prudent. She is aware that there can be no happiness where duty has been left undone, and that loving-kindness is a main source of felicity. Hence she is attentive to duty, and she practises the altruism which is at once the cause and the result of loving-kindness. She deliberately cultivates cheerfulness and resignation ; she discourages discontent as gardeners discourage a weed. She has duly noted that the kingdom of heaven is 'within you,' not near the band at the expensive restaurant, nor in the trying-on room of the fashionable dressmaker's next door to the expensive restaurant, nor in the *salons* of the well-advertised great. Her life is reflected in her face, which is a much better face than the face of the social butterfly. Whatever may occur—within reason—she is armed against destiny, married or single.

III

What can there be in common between these two types? Well, the point I am coming to is that they may have one tragic similarity which vitiates their lives equally, or almost equally. One may be vastly more admirable than the other, and in many matters vastly more sensible. And yet they may both have made the same stupendous mistake: the misinterpretation of the significance of the word happiness. Towards the close of existence, and even throughout existence, the second, in spite of all her precautions, may suffer the secret and hidden pangs of unhappiness just as acutely as the first; and her career may in the end present itself to her as just as much a sham.

And for the same reason. The social butterfly was running after something absurd, and the other woman knew that it was absurd and left it alone. But the root of the matter was more profound. The social butterfly's chief error was not that she was running after something, but that she was running away from something—something which I have described as mysterious and sinister. And the other woman also may be—and as a fact frequently is—running away from just that mysterious and sinister something. And that something is neither more nor less than life itself in its every essence. Both may be afraid of life and may have to pay an equal price for their cowardice. Both may have refused to listen to the voice within them, and will suffer equally for the wilful shutting of the ear.

(It is true that the other woman may just possibly have a true vocation for a career of resignation and altruism, and the spreading of a sort of content in a thin layer over the entire length of existence. If so, well and good. But it is also true that the social butterfly may have a true vocation for being a social butterfly, and the thick squandering of a sort of pleasure on the earlier part of existence, to the deprivation of the latter part. Then neither the one nor the other will have been guilty of the cowardice of running away from life.)

My point is that you may take refuge in good works or you may take refuge in bad works, but that the supreme offence against life lies in taking refuge from it, and that if you commit this offence you will miss the only authentic happiness—which springs no more from content and resignation than it springs from mere pleasure. It is indisputable that the conscience can be, and is constantly narcotised as much by relatively good deeds as by relatively bad deeds. Nevertheless, to dope the conscience is always a crime, and is always punished by the ultimate waking up of the conscience.

IV

To take refuge from life is to refuse it. Life generally offers due scope for the leading instinct in a man or a woman ; and sometimes it offers the scope at a very low price, at no price at all.

For example, a young man may have a very marked instinct for engineering, and his father may be a celebrated and wealthy engineer who is only too anxious that the son should follow the same profession. Life has offered the scope and charged nothing for it.

But, on the other hand, a man may have a very marked instinct for authorship, and his father may be a celebrated and wealthy engineer who, being convinced that literature is an absurd and despicable profession, has determined that his son shall not be an author but an engineer. 'Become an engineer,' says the father, 'and I will give you unique help, and you are a made man. Become an author, and you get nothing whatever from me except opposition.'

Life, however, which has provided the instinct for literature, has also provided the scope for its fulfilment. The scope for young authors is vaster to-day on two continents than ever it was. But the price which in this case life quotes is very high. The young man hesitates. The price quoted includes comfort, parental approval, domestic peace, money, luxury, and perhaps also a comfortable and not unsatisfactory marriage. It includes practically all the ingredients of the mixture commonly known as happiness. Of course, by following literature the young man may recover all and more than all the price paid. But also he may not. The chances are about a hundred to one that he will not. He is risking nearly everything in order to buy a ticket in a lottery.

Let us say that, being a prudent and obedient young fellow, he declines to beggar himself for a ticket in a lottery. His instinct towards literature has not developed very far; he sacrifices it and becomes the engineer. By industry and goodwill and native brains he becomes a very fair engineer, the prop of the firm, the aid, and in due course the successor, of his father. He treats his work-people well. He marries a delightful girl, and he even treats her well. He has delightful children. He is a terrific worldly success, and a model to his fellow-creatures. That man's attention to duty, his altruism, his real kindness, are the theme of conversation among all his friends. He treats his conscience with the most extraordinary respect.

And yet, if his instinct towards literature was genuine, he is not fundamentally happy, and when he chances to meet an author, or to read about authors (even about their suicides of despair), or to be deeply impressed by a book, he is acutely aware that he has committed the sin of taking refuge from life ; he knows that the extraordinary respect which he pays to his conscience is at bottom a doping of that organ ; he perceives that the smooth path is in fact the rough path, and that the rough path, which he dared not face, might have been, with all its asperities, th. smooth one. His existence is a vast secret and poisonous regret ; and there is nothing whatever to be done ; there is no antidote for the poison ; the dope is a drug—and insufficient at that.

V

Women, even in these latter days when reason is supposed to have got human nature by the neck, have far greater opportunities and temptations than men to run away from life. Indeed, many of them are taught and encouraged to do so. The practice of the three ancient cardinal female virtues—shutting your eyes, stopping your ears, and burying your head in the sand—is very carefully inculcated; and then, of course, people turn round on young women and upbraid them because they are afraid of existence! And, though things are changing, they have not yet definitely changed. I would not blame a whole sex—no matter which—for anything whatever. But to state a fact is not to blame. The fact is that women, when they get a chance, do show a tendency to shirk life. Large numbers of them come to grips with life simply because they are compelled to do so. A woman whose material existence is well assured will not as a rule go out into the world. Further, she will not marry as willingly as the woman who needs a home and cannot see the prospect of it except through marriage. By which I mean to imply that with women the achievement of marriage is due less to the instinct to mate than to an economic instinct. Men are wicked animals and know not righteousness, but it may be said of them generally that with them the achievement of marriage *is* due to the instinct to mate.

Examining the cases of certain women who put off marrying, I have been forced to the conclusion that their only reason for hesitating to marry is that men are not perfect, and that to marry an imperfect man involves risk. It does, but the reason is not valid. Risk is the very essence of life, and the total absence of danger is equal to death. I do not say that to follow an unsatisfactory vocation and to fail in it is better than to follow no vocation. But I am inclined to say that any marriage is better than no marriage—for both sexes. And I think that the most tragic spectacle on earth is an old woman metaphorically wrapped in cotton-wool who at some period of her career has refused life because of the peril of inconvenience and unhappiness.

Both men and women can run away from life in ways far more subtle and less drastic than those which I have named. For the sake of clearness I have confined myself to rather crude and obvious examples of flight. There are probably few of us who are not conscious of having declined at least some minor challenge of existence. And there are still fewer of us who can charge ourselves with having been consistently too bold in our desire to get the full savour of existence.

VI

Each individual must define happiness for himself or herself. For my part, I rule out practically all the dictionary definitions. In most dictionaries you will find that the principal meaning attached to the word is 'good fortune' or 'prosperity.' Which is notoriously absurd. Then come such definitions as 'a state of well-being characterised by relative permanence, by dominantly agreeable emotion . . . and by a natural desire for its continuation.' This last is from Webster, and it is very clever. Yet I will have none of it, unless I am allowed to define the word 'well-being' in my own way.

For me, an individual cannot be in a state of well-being if any of his faculties are permanently idle through any fault of his own. The full utilisation of all the faculties seems to me to be the foundation of well-being. But I doubt if a full utilisation of all the faculties necessarily involves the idea of good fortune, or prosperity, or tranquillity, or contentedness with one's lot, or even a 'dominantly agreeable emotion'; very often it rather involves the contrary.

In my view happiness includes chiefly the idea of 'satisfaction after full honest effort.' Everybody is guilty of mistakes and of serious mistakes, and the contemplation of these mistakes must darken, be it ever so little, the last years of existence. But it need not be fatal to a general satisfaction. Men and women may in the end be forced to admit: 'I made a fool of myself,' and still be fairly happy. But no one can possibly be satisfied, and therefore no one can in my sense be happy, who feels that in some paramount affair he has failed to take up the challenge of life. For a voice within him, which none else can hear,

RUNNING AWAY FROM LIFE

but which he cannot choke, will constantly be murmuring :

'You lacked courage. You hadn't the pluck. You ran away.'

And it is happier to be unhappy in the ordinary sense all one's life than to have to listen at the end to that dreadful interior verdict.

SOME AXIOMS ABOUT WAR-WORK

SOME AXIOMS ABOUT WAR-WORK

I

THIS essay concerns men, but it concerns women more.

When citizens begin to learn, through newspapers and general rumour, that voluntary war-work is afoot, and that volunteers are badly wanted, and that there is work for all who love their country, then those who love their country are at once sharply divided into two classes—the people to whom the work comes, and the people who have to go out to seek the work. The former are the people of prominent social position; the latter are the remainder of the population. The prominent persons will see work rolling up to their front doors in quantities huge enough to overthrow the entire house. The remainder will look out of the window and see nothing at all unusual in the street. They are then apt to say : ' This is very odd. There is much work to do. I am ready to do my share. Why doesn't somebody come along and ask me to do it ? ' And they feel rather hurt at the neglect, and finally they sigh : ' Well, if no one gives me anything to do, of course I can't do anything.'

Such an attitude would be quite reasonable if society was like a telephone-exchange, and anybody could get precisely the person he or she was after by paying a girl a pound or two a week to stick plugs into holes. But society not being like a telephone-exchange, the attitude is unreasonable. Patriots cannot expect the organisers of war-work to run up and down streets knocking at doors and crying : ' Come ! You are the very woman

SOME AXIOMS ABOUT WAR-WORK

I need!' However much urgent war-work is waiting to be done, nine-tenths of the individuals who are anxious to do it will have to put themselves to a certain amount of trouble in order to discover the work, perhaps to a great deal of trouble. Having located the work, they may even have almost to beg for the privilege of doing it. Again, they are rather hurt. They demand, why should they go on their knees? They are not asking a favour.

A woman will say:

'I went and offered my services. And he looked at me as if I was a doubtful character, and you never heard such a cross-examination as I had to go through! It was most humiliating.'

True! True! But could she reasonably expect the cross-examiner to see into the inside of her head? The first use and the last use of the gift of speech is to ask questions.

Moreover, respected madam, it is quite probable that the cross-examiner was not a bit suspicious, and that his manner was simply due to dumbfoundedness, to mere inability to believe that so ideal a person as yourself had, so to speak, fallen from heaven straight into his net. And further, respected madam, are not you yourself suspicious? If the cross-examiner had come to you, instead of you going to him, might not your first thought have been: 'What advantage is he trying to gain by coming to me? I shall say No!' If it is true that people who ask for work are stared at, it is equally true that people who are asked to work also stare—a little haughtily. And when the latter graciously promise assistance, they often say to themselves: 'I shall do as little as I can, because I'm not going to be taken advantage of.' And they almost invariably end by doing more than they can, and by insisting on being taken advantage of. Human nature is mean, but it is also noble.

Axiom : The preliminary trouble and weariness and annoyance incidental to getting the work are themselves a necessary and inevitable part of war-work, just as much as bandaging the brows of heroes.

II

Life is a continual passage from one illusion to another. No sooner has the eager volunteer found out that the desire to help is apt to be treated as evidence of a criminal disposition, and that war-work is as shy as deer in the depths of a forest—no sooner has he or she discovered these things than yet another discovery destroys yet another illusion. The war-work when brought to bay and caught is not the right kind of war-work. You—for I may as well admit that I am talking direct to the eager volunteer—you had expected something else. This war-work that presents itself is either beneath your powers, or it is beyond your powers; or it is unsuited to your individuality or to your social station or to your health or to your hands or feet. You can scarcely say what you had expected, but at any rate . . . I will tell you what you had expected. You had expected the ideal—work that showed you at your best, picturesque work, interesting work, work free from monotony, work of which you could see the immediate beautiful results, work which taxed you without overtaxing you, really important work without the moral risks attaching to real responsibility. Such was the work you had expected, and the chances are ten to one that the work you have actually got is dull, monotonous, apparently futile; any fool could do it, though it is exhausting and inconvenient. Or, on the other hand, it is, while dull and monotonous, too exacting

SOME AXIOMS ABOUT WAR-WORK

for a well-intentioned mediocre brain like yours (you don't actually mean that, but you try to be modest)—in short it is not suitable work.

Axiom: There is not enough suitable work to go round, nor the thousandth part of what would be enough. Unsuitableness is a characteristic of nearly all war-work. Lowering your great powers down, or forcing your little powers up, to the level of the work offered—this, too, is part of war-work.

III

Again, you have to get away from the illusion that you can live a new life and still keep on living the old life. Everybody, as has somewhere been stated, possesses twenty-four hours in each day. Everybody occupies every one of his twenty-four hours. You do, though you may think you don't. If you do not occupy them in labour then you occupy them in idleness; if not in usefulness, then in futility. Now idleness and futility are much more difficult to expel from hours which they have appropriated than labour and usefulness are difficult to expel. But if war-work is brought in, something will have to be expelled. Habits of labour and usefulness are sometimes hard enough to change; habits of idleness and futility are still harder. If you were previously spending your afternoons in giving and accepting elaborate afternoon teas, you will have more trouble in devoting your afternoons to war-work than if you had been spending them, for example, in the pursuit of knowledge. It is child's play to abandon the pursuit of knowledge; no moral stamina is required; but to give up the exciting sociabilities of afternoon tea is a tremendous feat. So much so, that if you are a votary of this indigestive practice, you will infallibly endeavour to persuade yourself

SOME AXIOMS ABOUT WAR-WORK

at first : 'I can manage the two—war-work and afternoon teas as well. I can fit them in.'

You cannot fit them in—at any rate successfully. The essence of war-work is that it may not be fitted in. If it does not mean sacrifice, it means naught. Sacrifice is giving something for nothing. You cannot give something and yet stick to it. Certain persons are apt to buy an article to give away, and then are so pleased with the article that they decide to keep it for themselves. They thus obtain for a period the sensation of benevolence without any ultimate corresponding sacrifice. This is the nearest approach, that I know of, to giving something and yet sticking to it ; but it has no relation whatever to war-work.

Axiom : If a tea-cup is full you cannot pour anything into it until you have poured something out.

IV

The next, and the next to the last, illusion to go is a masterpiece of simple-mindedness, and yet nearly all who take up war-work are found at first to be under its sway. It is the illusion that war-work, being a fine and noble thing, ought to change people's natures and dispositions, in such a manner as to produce the maximum of co-operating effort with the minimum of friction.

Now the very heart of all war-work is the grand and awe-inspiring institution of the Committee. If you are engaged on war-work you are bound to sit on a Committee; or, in default of a Committee, a Sub-Committee (which usually has more real power than the bumptious and unwieldy body that overlords it). And, if you are on neither a Committee nor a Sub-Committee, then you are bound sooner or later to be called up before a Committee or a Sub-Committee, and to be in a position to give the Committee or Sub-Committee a piece of your mind. Thus your legitimate ambition will somehow be satisfied.

But let us suppose that you are at once elected to a Committee. Well, among the members of the Committee are three persons you know—Miss X, Mr. Y, and Mrs. Z. Miss X used to be a mannish and reckless and cheeky young maid. Mr. Y used to be an interfering and narrow-minded old maid. Mrs. Z used to be nothing in particular. You enter the Committee-room, and you see these three, together with a few others who have not a very promising air. (Probably no sight is more depressing than the cordon of faces round a Committee-room table.) You, however, are not downcast. You feel in yourself the uplifting power of a great ideal. You are determined to make the best of yourself and of everybody. And you are convinced that everybody is determined to do the same. But in less than five minutes Miss X, despite her obvious lack of experience, is offering the most absurd proposals ; she has put her elbows on the table ; and she is calmly teaching all her grandmothers to suck eggs. Mr. Y is objecting to the ruling of the Chairman, and obstinately arguing against a resolution that has been carried, and indeed implying that the Committee ought not to do anything at all. As for Mrs. Z she has scarcely opened her mouth ; when the Chairman asked her for her opinion she blushed and said she rather agreed, and she voted both for and against the first resolution.

' Is it conceivable,' you exclaim in your soul, ' is it conceivable that these individuals can behave so in such a supreme crisis of the nation's history, at a moment when the nation has need of every citizen's loyal goodwill, of every—?' etc. etc. 'No! They cannot have realised that we are at war!'

And sundry other members of the Committee are not much better than the ignoble three. Indeed, your faith in Committees is practically destroyed. You say to yourself, with your blunt, vigorous common sense: 'If only the Committee would adjourn and leave the whole matter to me, I am sure I could manage it much better than they are doing.' You consider that a Committee is a device for wasting time and for flattering the conceit of opinionated fools. . . . Then Mr. Y becomes absolutely impossible. You feel that you are prepared to stand a lot, but that there is a limit and that Mr. Y has gone beyond it. You are ready to work, and to work hard, but you cannot be expected to work with people who are impossible. You decide to send in your resignation to the Chairman at once.

I hope you will not send it in. For at least half the Committee are thinking just as you are thinking. And one or two of them are thinking these things, not apropos of Miss X, Mr. Y, or Mrs. Z, but apropos of you! And if you are startled at the spectacle of people persisting in being just themselves in war-work, then the fault is yours, and you should be gently ashamed. You ought to have known that people are never more themselves than in a great crisis, especially when the crisis is prolonged. You ought to be thankful that the Committee has unscaled your eyes to so fundamental a truth. You have realised that we are at war,—you ought also to realise that it takes all sorts to make a world, even a world at war. You ought to imagine what would happen if every member of the Committee, like you, resigned because Mr. Y was impossible, and thus left the impossible Mr.

SOME AXIOMS ABOUT WAR-WORK

Y in possession of the table and the secretary.

Axiom : The most valorous and morally valuable war-work is the work of working with impossible people.

And may I warn you that you will later on, if you succeed as a war-worker, encounter more terrible phenomena than Mr. Y, who at the worst can always be out-voted ? You will encounter, for example, the famous and fashionable lady who, justifiably relying on human nature's profound and incurable snobbishness, will give all the hard work to you and those like you, while appropriating all the glory and advertisement for herself. And, more terrible even than the famous and fashionable lady, you will run up against the Official Mind. The Official Mind is the worst of all obstacles to getting things done. And the gravest danger of the war-worker, particularly if he attains high rank on Com-

40 SELF AND SELF-MANAGEMENT

mittees, is the danger of becoming official-minded himself.

V

When you have proved that in war-work you are a decent human being—and you will prove this by sticking to the work long after you are weary of it, and by refusing to fly off to something else because it promises to be more diverting and less annoying than your present job—then you will part company with the war-workers' last illusion. Namely, the illusion that her efforts will meet with gratitude. Gratitude is going to be an extremely rare commodity, and it is not a very good thing to receive, anyhow. You see, there will be so few people with leisure to devote to gratitude. Everybody is or will be war-working. Even soldiers and sailors are doing something for the war, though to listen to some civilians one would suppose the military side of war to be relatively quite unimportant. No ! Gratitude will not choke the market. On the contrary, criticism will be rife, for we are all experts in war-work. The highest hope of the average war-worker must be to escape censure. Official food-controllers, who are possibly the supreme type of war-worker, are thankful if they escape with their heads. And herein is a great lesson.

Axiom : The reward of war-work will be in the treaty of peace.

THE DIARY HABIT

THE DIARY HABIT

I

LET us consider, first, a strange quality of the written word.

The spoken word is bad enough. Such things as misfortunes, blunders, sins, and apprehensions become more serious when they have been described even in conversation. A woman who secretly fears cancer will fear it much more once she has mentioned her fear to another person. The spoken word has somehow given reality to her fear. But the written word is far more formidable than the spoken word. It is said that the ignorant and the uncultured have a superstitious dread of writing. The dread is not superstitious; it is based on a mysterious and intimidating phenomenon which nearly anybody can test for himself. The fact is that almost all people are afraid of writing—I mean true, honest writing. Vast numbers of people hate and loathe it, as though it were a high explosive that might suddenly go off and blow them to pieces. (That is one reason why realistic novels never have a very large sale.) But the difference between one man's dread of writing and another man's dread of writing is merely a difference of degree, not of kind. And if any among you asserts that he has no fear of the written word, merely because it is written, let him try the following experiment.

Take—O exceptional individual!—take some concealed and blameworthy action or series of thoughts of your own. I do not mean necessarily murder or embezzlement; not everybody has committed murder or embezzlement, or even desires to do so; I mean some matter—any matter—of which

THE DIARY HABIT

you are so ashamed, or about which you are so nervous, that you have never mentioned it to a soul. All of us—even you—have such matters hidden beneath waistcoat or corsage. Write down that matter; put it in black and white. The chances are that you won't; the chances are that you will find some excuse for not writing it down.

You may say:

'Ah! But suppose some one happened to see it!'

To which I would reply:

'Write it and lock it up in your safe.'

To which you may rejoin:

'Ah! But I might lose the key of the safe and some one might find it and open the safe. Also I might die suddenly.'

To which I would retort:

'If you are dead you needn't mind discovery.'

To which you might respond:

'How do you know that if I was dead I needn't mind discovery?'

Well, I will yield you that point, and still prove to you that your objection to the written word does not spring from the fear of giving yourself away. The experiment shall be performed under strict conditions.

Empty your house of all its inhabitants save yourself. Lock the front-door and the back-door. Go upstairs to your own room. Lock the door of your own room. Pile furniture before the door, so that you cannot possibly be surprised. Light a fire. Place the writing-table near the fire. Arrange it so that at the slightest alarm of discovery you can with a single movement thrust your writing into the fire. Then begin to write down that of which you are ashamed. You are absolutely safe. Nevertheless you will hesitate to write. And you will not have got very far in your narration before you find yourself writing down something that is not quite so unpleasant as the truth, or before you find yourself omitting some detail which ought not to be omitted. You will have great difficulty in forcing yourself to be utterly frank on paper. You may fail in being utterly frank; you probably will so fail; most people do. When you have finished and hold the document in your hand, you will start guiltily if the newly moved furniture creaks in front of the door. You will read through the document with discomfort and constraint. And you will stick it in the fire and watch it burn with a very clear feeling of relief.

Why all these strange sensations? You could not have been caught in the act. Moreover, there was nothing on the paper of which you were not fully aware, and which you had not fully realised. Nobody can write down that which he does not know and realise.

Quite possibly the whole matter had been thoroughly familiar to you, a commonplace of your brain, for weeks, months, years. Quite possibly you had recalled every detail of it hundreds of times, and it had never caused you any grave inconvenience. But, instantly it is written down it becomes acutely, intolerably disturbing—so much so that you cannot rest until the written word is destroyed. You are precisely the same man as you were before beginning to write ; naught is altered ; you have committed no new crime. But you have a new shame. I repeat, why ? The only immediate answer is that the honest written word possesses a mysterious and intimidating power. This power has to do with the sense of sight. You see something. You do not see your action or your thoughts as it might be on the cinema screen —happily !—but you do see *something* in regard to the matter.

THE DIARY HABIT

II

The above considerations are offered to that enormous class of people, springing up afresh every year, who say to themselves: 'I will keep a diary and it shall be absolutely true.' You may keep a diary, but beyond question it will not be absolutely true. You will be lucky, or you must be rather gifted, if it is not studded with untruths. You protest that you have a well-earned reputation for veracity. I would not doubt it. When I say 'untruths' I do not mean, for instance, that if the day was beautifully fine you would write in your diary: 'A very wet day to-day; went for a walk and got soaked through.' I am convinced that you would be above such lying perversions. But also I am convinced that if a husband and wife, both as veracious and conscientious as yourself, had a quarrel and described the history of the quarrel each in a private diary, the two accounts would by no means coincide, and the whole truth would be in neither of them. Some people start a diary as casually as they start golf, stamps, or a new digestive cure. Whereas to start a diary ought to be a solemn and notable act, done with a due appreciation of the difficulties thereby initiated. The very essence of a diary is truth—a diary of untruth would be pointless—and to attain truth is the hardest thing on earth. To attain partial truth is not a bit easy, and even to avoid falsehood is decidedly a feat.

III

Having discouraged, I now wish to encourage. Many who want to keep diaries and who ought to keep diaries do not, because they are too diffident. They say : ' My life is not interesting enough.' I ask : ' Interest-

THE DIARY HABIT 53

ing to whom? To the world in general or to themselves?' It is necessary only that a life should be interesting to the person who lives that life. If you have a desire to keep a diary, it follows that your existence is interesting to you. Otherwise obviously you would not wish to make a record of it. The greatest diarists did not lead very palpitating lives. Ninety-five per cent. of *Pepys's Diary* deals with tiny daily happenings of the most banal sort—such happenings as we all go through. If Pepys re-read his entries the day after he wrote them, he must have found them somewhat tedious. Certainly he had not the slightest notion that he was writing one of the great outstanding books of English literature.

But diaries are the opposite of novels, in that time increases instead of decreasing their interest. After a reasonable period every sentence in a diary blossoms into interest, and the diarist simply cannot be dull—any more than a great wit such as Sidney Smith could be unfunny. If Sidney Smith asked Helen to pass him the salt, the entire table roared with laughter because it was inexplicably so funny. If the diarist writes in his diary, ' I asked Helen to pass me the salt,' within three years he will find the sentence inexplicably interesting to himself. In thirty years his family will be inexplicably interested to read that on a certain day he asked Helen to pass him the salt. In three hundred years a whole nation will be reading with inexplicable and passionate interest that centuries earlier he asked Helen to pass him the salt, and critics will embroider theories upon both Helen and the salt and will even earn a living by producing new annotated editions of Helen and the salt. And if the diary turns up after three thousand years, the entire world will hum with the inexplicable thrilling fact that

THE DIARY HABIT

he asked Helen to pass him the salt; which fact will be cabled round the globe as a piece of latest news; and immediately afterwards there will be cabled round the globe the views of expert scholars of all nationalities on the problem whether, when he had asked Helen to pass him the salt, Helen did actually pass him the salt, or not. Timid prospective diarists in need of encouragement should keep this great principle in mind.

You will say :

'But what do I care about posterity? I would not keep a diary for the sake of posterity.'

Possibly not, but some people would. Some people, if they thought their diaries would be read three hundred years hence, or even a hundred years hence, would begin diaries to-morrow and persevere with them to the day of death. Some people of course are peculiar. And I admit that I am of your opinion. The thought of posterity leaves me stone cold.

There is only one valid reason for beginning a diary—namely, that you find pleasure in beginning it; and only one valid reason for continuing a diary—namely, that you find pleasure in continuing it. You may find profit in doing so, but that is not the main point—though it is a point. You will most positively experience pleasure in reading it after a long interval; but that is not the main point either—though it is an important point. A diary should find its sufficient justification in the writing of it. If the act of writing is not its own reward, then let the diary remain for ever unwritten.

IV

But beware of that word 'writing.' Just as some persons are nervous when entering a drawing-room (or even a restaurant !), so

THE DIARY HABIT 57

some persons are nervous when taking up a pen. All persons, as I have tried to show, are nervous about the psychological effects of the written word, but some persons—indeed many—are additionally nervous about the mere business of writing the word. They begin to hanker, with awe, after a mysterious ideal known as 'correct style.' They are actually under the delusion that writing is essentially different from talking—a secret trade process !—and they are not aware that he who says or thinks interesting things can write interesting things, and that he who can make himself understood in speech can make himself understood in writing—if he goes the right way to work !

I have known people, especially the young, who could discourse on themselves in the most attractive manner for hours, and yet who simply could not discover in their heads sufficient material for a short letter. They would bemoan : 'I can't think of anything to say.' It was true. And, of course, they could not think of anything to *say*, the reason being that they were trying to think of something to *write*, and very wrongly assuming that writing is necessarily different from saying ! Writing may be different from saying, but it need not be different, and for the diarist it should not be different. And, above all, it should not be superficially different. The inexperienced, when they use ink, have a pestilent notion that saying has to be translated or transmogrified into writing. They conceive an idea in spoken words, and then they subconsciously or consciously ask themselves : 'I should say it like that—but how ought I to write it ?' They alter the forms of their sentences. They worry about grammar and phrase-construction and even spelling. As for grammar and spelling, in the greatest age of English litera-

THE DIARY HABIT

ture neither subject was understood, and no writer could be trusted either in spelling or in grammar. To this day very few writers of genius are to be trusted either in spelling or in grammar. As for phrase-construction, the phrase that comes to your tongue is more likely to be well constructed than the phrase which you bring forcibly into being at the point of your pen. If you know enough grammar to talk comprehensibly, you know enough to write comprehensibly, and you need not trouble about anything else; in fact, you ought not to do so, and you must not. Formality in a diary is a mistake. Write as you think, as you speak, and it may be given to you to produce literature. But if while you are writing you remember that there is such a thing as literature, you will assuredly never produce literature.

This does not mean that you are entitled to write anyhow, without thought and without effort. Not a bit. Good diaries are not achieved thus. Although you may and should ignore the preoccupations of what I will call, sarcastically, ' literary composition,' you must have always before you the ideal of effectively getting your thought on to the paper. You would, sooner or later, *say* your thought effectively, but in writing it down some travail is needed to imagine what the perhaps unstudied spoken words would be. And also, the memory must be fully and honestly exercised to recall the scene or the incident described. By carelessness you run the risk of ' leaving out the interesting part.' By being conscientious you ensure that the maximum of interest is attained.

Lastly, it is necessary to conquer the human objection to hard labour of any sort. It is not a paradox to assert that man often dislikes the work which he likes. For myself, every day anew, I hate to start work.

THE DIARY HABIT

You may end your day with the full knowledge that you have had experiences that day worthy to go into the diary, which experiences remain in your mind obstinately. And yet you hate to open the diary, and even when you have opened it you hate to put your back into the business of writing. You are tempted to write without reflection, without order, and too briefly. To resist the temptation to be slack and casual and second-rate involves constant effort. Diary-keeping should be a pastime, but properly done it is also a task—like many other pastimes. I have kept a diary for over twenty-one years, and I know a little about it. I know more than a little about the remorse—alas, futile!—which follows negligence. In diary-keeping negligence cannot be repaired. That which is gone is gone beyond return.

A DANGEROUS LECTURE
TO A YOUNG WOMAN

A DANGEROUS LECTURE
TO A YOUNG WOMAN

I

IT was at a war-charity sale, in a hot, crowded public room of a fashionable hotel, amid the humorous bellowings of an amateur auctioneer and the guffaws of amused bidders, that this thing happened to me. A young woman was passing, and, as she passed, she looked and stopped, and abruptly charged me with being myself. I admitted the undeniable.

'I hope you'll excuse me,' she said. 'I've read all your books.'

'The usual amiable chatter,' I thought, and made aloud my usual, stilted, self-conscious reply to such a conversational opening:

'You must have worked very hard.'

She frowned—just a little frown in the middle of her forehead. She was very well-dressed (which is not a fault), and she had a pleasant, sympathetic, serious face. She said :

' I 've often wanted to tell you ; in fact, I thought I ought to tell you about all those little books of yours about life and improving oneself, and being efficient and not wasting time, and so on, and so on. They 're very nice to read, but they 've never done me any good—practically.' She smiled.

(No ; it was not to be the usual amiable chatter !)

' I 'm sorry,' I said. ' But, of course, books don't act by themselves. You can't expect them to be of much practical good until you begin to put them into practice.'

' But that 's just the point,' she answered. ' I can't *begin* to put them into practice. I can't resolve, and I can't concentrate, and

I can't clench my teeth and make up my mind. And if I do make a sort of start, it's a failure after the first day. And this goes on year after year. No use blaming me—I can't help myself. I want awfully—but I can't.'

'But *what* do you want?'

'I want to make the best of myself. I want to stop wasting time and to perfect my "human machine." I want to succeed in life. I want to live properly and bring out all my faculties. Only, you see, I haven't got any resolution. I simply have not got it in me. You tell me to make up my mind, steel myself, resolve, stick to it, and so forth. Well, I just can't. And yet I do want to. You've never dealt with my case—and, what's more, I don't think you can deal with it. I hope you'll pardon all this bluntness. But I thought that, as a student of human nature, you might be interested.'

I stood silent for a moment. She bowed with much charm and fled away. I gazed everywhere. But she was lost in the huge room. I could not very well run in pursuit of her—these things are not done in literary circles. She had vanished. And I knew naught of her. She might be young girl, young wife, young mother, anything—but I knew naught of her except that she had a sympathetic, rather sad face, and that she had left an arrow quivering in my side.

II

A few hours later, however, I spoke to the young creature as follows :

'It seems to me that you may have been running your delightful head up against an impossible proposition. Perhaps you have been hoping to *create* energy in yourself. Now, you cannot create energy, either in yourself or elsewhere. Nobody can. You can only set energy free, loosen it, transform it, direct it.

'You may take a ton of coal and warm a house with it. The heat-energy of the coal is transformed, set free, and directed to a certain purpose. But if you try to warm the house by means of open coal fires in old-fashioned fire-grates, you will warm the chimneys and some of the air above the chimneys—and yet the rooms of the house will not be appreciably warmer than they were when you began. On the other hand, you may take a ton of exactly the same kind of coal and by means of a steam-heating system in the cellar warm the rooms of the house to such an extent that you have to wear your summer clothes in the depth of winter. The steam-heating system, however, has not increased the heat-energy of the coal; it has merely set free, utilised, and directed the heat-energy of the coal in a common-sense—that is to say, a scientific—manner. No amount of common sense and ingenuity will get as much heat-energy out of half a ton as out of a ton of coal. You may devise the most marvellous steam-heating system that exists on this side of the grave, but if there is no fuel in the furnace, or if there is in the furnace a quantity of coal inadequate to the size of the house, the house will never be comfortable except for polar bears and lovers. The available coal is the prime factor.

'Well, an individual is born with a certain amount of energy—and no more. Just as you cannot pour five quarts out of a gallon (as a rule, you cannot pour even four quarts), so you cannot extract from that individual more energy than there is in him. And, what is more important, you cannot put additional quantities of energy into him. You may sometimes seem to be putting energy into him, but you are not; you are simply setting his original energy free, applying a match to the coal or fanning the fire. An individual is an island on whose rocky shores no ship can ever land that most mysterious commodity—energy. You may transfuse blood, but not the inexplicable force that makes the heart beat and defies circumstance.

'Some individuals appear to lack energy, when, as a fact, they are full of energy which is merely dormant, waiting for the match, or waiting for direction. Other individuals appear to lack energy, and, in fact, do lack energy. And you cannot supply their need any more than you can stop their hair from growing.

'No, young lady ; it is useless to interrupt me by asking me to define what I mean by the word " energy." To define some words is to cripple them. You know well enough what I mean by energy. I mean the most fundamental thing in you.

'Being a reasonable woman, you admit this—and then go on to demand, first, how you can be quite sure whether you have been born with a large or medium or a small quantity of energy, and, second, how you can be quite sure that you have not lots of energy lying dormant within you. You cannot be quite sure of anything. This is not a perfect world.

'But, as regards the second part of your question, you can be reasonably sure after a certain number of years—I will not suggest how many—that energy is not lying dormant within you, awaiting the match. It is impossible for anybody indefinitely to continue to wander in a world full of lighted matches without one day encountering the particular match that will set fire to *his* fuel. And beware of that match, for sometimes the result of the contact is an explosion which shatters everything in the vicinity. If you have dormant energy, one day it will wake

A DANGEROUS LECTURE

up and worry you, and you will know it is there.

'As regards the first part of your question, the usual index of the amount of energy possessed by an individual is the intensity of the desires of that individual. It is desire that uses energy. Strong desires generally betoken much energy, and they are definite desires. Without desires, energy is rendered futile. Nobody will consume energy in action unless he desires to perform the action, either for itself or as a means to a desired end.

'But now you complain that I am once more avoiding your case. You assert that you have desires without the corresponding energy or corresponding will to put them into execution. I doubt it. I do not admit it. You must not confuse vague, general aspirations with desire. A real desire is definite, concrete. If you have a real desire, you know what you want. You cannot merely want—you are bound to want something.

'Further, to want something only at intervals, when the mind is otherwise unoccupied, is no proof of a real desire; it amounts to nothing more than a sweet, sad diversion, a spiritual pastime, a simple and pleasant way of making yourself believe that you are a serious person. The desire which indicates great energy is always there, worrying. It is an obsession; it is a nuisance; it is a whip and a scorpion; it has no mercy.

'And individuals having immense energy have commonly been actuated by a single paramount desire, which monopolises and canalises all their force. The pity is that these individuals have become the special symbols of success. When they have achieved their single paramount desire, they are said to have " got on," to have succeeded. And every one points an admiring finger at them and cries, "This is success in life!" And the majority of books about success in life deal with this particular brand of success, and assume that it is the only brand of success worth a bilberry, and exhort all people to imitate the notorious exemplars of the art of "getting on" and in that narrow sense. Which is absurd.

'And now, perhaps, we both feel that I am at last approaching your case.

'But I do not wish to be personal. Let us take the case of Mr. Flack, who died last week, unknown. His discerning friends said of him: "He had a wonderful financial gift. If he'd concentrated on it, he might have rivalled Harriman. But he wouldn't concentrate either on that or on anything else. He was interested in too many different subjects — books, pictures, music, travel, physical science, love, economics—in fact, everything interested him, and he was always interested in something. He was too all-round. He frittered his energy away, and wasted enormous quantities of time. And so he never succeeded."

'Such was the verdict of some of Flack's admirers. But it occurs to me that Flack may have succeeded after all. Certainly he did not succeed in being a financial magnate. But he succeeded in being interested in a large number of things, and therefore in having a wide mind. He succeeded in being always interested. And he succeeded in not being lop-sided, which men of one supreme desire as a rule are. (Men who are successful in the narrow sense generally pay a fearful price for their success.) His friends regret that he wasted his time, but really, if he accomplished all that he admittedly did accomplish, he couldn't have wasted a very great deal of time.

A DANGEROUS LECTURE

'Quite possibly the late Mr. Flack used to wake up in the night and curse himself because he could not concentrate, and because he could not stick to one thing, and because he wasted his time, and because, with all his gifts, he did not materially progress, and because he made no impression on the great public. Quite possibly, in moments of gloom, he had regrets about the dissipation of his energy. But he could not honestly have regarded himself as a failure.

'I should like to know why it is necessarily more righteous to confine one's energy to a single direction than to let it spread out in various directions. It is not more righteous. If a man has one imperious desire, his righteousness is to satisfy it fully. But if a man has many mild, equal desires, *his* righteousness is to satisfy all of them as reasonably well as circumstances permit. And I see no reason why one should be deemed more successful than the other.

'Yes, young woman; I know what your excellent modesty is going to say. It is going to say that the late Mr. Flack did show energy, though he "frittered it away," and that you do not show energy. Now, I do not want to defend you against yourself (for possibly you enjoy denouncing yourself and proving that you are worthless). Nevertheless, I would point out that energy is often used in ways quite unsuspected. Energy is a very various thing. Some people use energy in arranging time-tables and sticking to them, and in clenching their teeth and making terrific resolves and executing them, and in never wasting a moment, and in climbing—climbing. And this is all very laudable. But energy can be used in other ways—in contemplation, in self-understanding, in understanding other people, in pleasing other people, in appreciating the world, in lessening the friction of life.

'I have personally come across persons —especially women—who were idle, who were mentally inefficient, who made no material contribution to the enterprise of remaining alive, but whose mere manner of existence was such that I would say to them in my heart, " It is enough for me that you exist."

'We have all of us come across such persons. And the world would be a markedly inferior sort of place if they did not exist exactly as they are.

'You, dear young woman, may or may not be one of these. I cannot decide. But, anyhow, if you are not one of the hard-striving, resolute, persevering, teeth-clenching, totally efficient, one-ideaed, ambitious species, you need not despair.

'Imagine what the world would be like if

we were all ruthlessly set on " succeeding " !
It would be like a scene of carnage. And
it is conceivable that you are, in fact, much
more efficient than you think, and that you
are wasting much less time than you think,
and that you are employing much more
energy than you think. You complained
that you lacked resolution, which means that
you lacked one steady desire. But perhaps
your steady desire and resolution are so in-
stinctive, so profoundly a part of you, that
they function without being noticed. And
if you do indeed lack one steady desire and
the energy firmly to resolve—well, you just
do. And you will have to be content with
your lot. Why envy others? An over-
mastering desire and its accompanying energy
are not necessarily to be envied.

'A dangerous doctrine, you say. You
say that I am leaving the door open to
sloth and slackness and other evils. You

A DANGEROUS LECTURE

say that I am finding an excuse for every unserious person under the sun. Perhaps so; but what I have said is true, and I will not be afraid of the truth because it happens to be dangerous. Moreover, every person ought to know in his heart whether or not he is conducting his existence satisfactorily. But he must interrogate his conscience fairly. It is not fair, either to one's conscience or to oneself, to listen to it always, for example, in the desolating dark hour before the dawn, and never to listen to it, for example, after one has had a good meal or a good slice of any sort of honest pleasure.

'And, lastly, I have mentioned envy. We are apt to mistake mere envy of the successful for an individual desire to succeed. Yet an envious realisation of all the advantages (and none of the disadvantages) of success is scarcely the same thing as a genuine instinct for " getting on "—is it?'

III

This long speech which I made to the young, dissatisfied creature might have been extremely effective if I could have made it to her face. I ought, however, to mention that I did not make it to her face. I have been reporting a harangue which I delivered in the sleepless middle of the night to her imagined image. It is easier to be effective in reply when the argumentative opponent is not present.

THE COMPLETE FUSSER

THE COMPLETE FUSSER

I

FREQUENTERS of lunatic asylums are familiar with the person who, being convinced that he is a poached egg, continually demands to be put on hot toast, and is continually unhappy because nobody will put him on hot toast. This man is quite harmless; he is merely a bore by reason of a ridiculous delusion about the fulfilment of his true destiny being bound up with hot toast; in character he is one of the most amiable individuals that ever lived, amiable even to the point of offering himself for consumption to those of his fellow-patients who are hungry, and who happen to fancy a poached egg with their tea. Nevertheless, on the score of his undeniable delusion he is segregated from ordinary society, and indeed imprisoned for life. Such may be the consequence of a delusion.

But not all deluded people are treated alike. A lady went for the week-end to stay in a country cottage. Now, this lady was accustomed to smoke a cigarette in her bath of a morning.

Let there be no mistake. She was a perfectly respectable lady. In former days respectable ladies neither smoked cigarettes nor took baths. The one habit was nearly as disreputable as the other. In the present epoch they do both with impunity, and though possibly a section of the public may consider that while for a woman to smoke a cigarette is quite nice, and for a woman to have a bath is quite nice, to smoke a cigarette in a bath is not quite nice for a woman, that section of the public is in a very small minority and should therefore be howled down.

THE COMPLETE FUSSER

Anyhow the lady in question was everything that a lady ought to be. She was in fact a well-known social worker and writer on social subjects. On the Sunday morning a terrible rumour was propagated throughout the country cottage. The lady did not smoke merely a cigarette in her bath—she smoked a special brand of cigarette in her bath. And she had forgotten to bring a due supply of the special brand, and her cigarette-case had been emptied on the previous night. It became known that she was in a fearful state, and would not be comforted. The brand was Egyptian. At first none but the brand would do for her, but after a period of agony she announced that she was ready to smoke any Egyptian or Turkish cigarette. The cottage, however, was neither Egyptian nor Turkish, but a Virginian cottage. She could not be induced to try a Virginian cigarette, and the cottage was miles from anywhere, and the day was the Sabbath.

She came downstairs miserable, unnerved, futile, a nuisance to herself and to her hosts. She could not discuss important social matters, which she had come on purpose to discuss. She could do naught except sympathise with herself, and this she did on a tremendous scale. In the afternoon a visitor called who possessed Egyptian cigarettes. The lady got one, and at the first puff was instantly restored to her normal condition. The hot toast had been brought to the poached egg.

The lady, I maintain, was suffering from a delusion at least as outrageous as the poached egg delusion, the delusion that her body and brain could not function properly —in other words that her destiny could not be fulfilled—unless she took into her mouth at a certain time a particular variety of gaseous fluid scarcely distinguishable from a thousand other similar varieties of gaseous fluid. Her physical perceptions were not at all delicate. Like most women, for example, she could not tell the difference between tea stewed and tea properly infused. If a Virginian cigarette had been falsely marked in an Egyptian manner she would have smoked it with gusto. And if she had been smoking in the dark she could not have told whether her cigarette was in or out—unless she inhaled.

The delusion was nothing but a delusion. Her mind, by a habitual process, had imagined it, and she had ended by being victimised by it. She had ended by seriously believing that she was physically and spiritually dependent upon a factor which had no appreciable power beyond the power mistakenly and insanely attributed to it by her morbid imagination.

But, did any one suggest that she ought to be confined in a lunatic asylum? Assuredly not. If ever she goes to a lunatic asylum it will be as a visitor, to smile superiorly at the man whose welfare depends utterly on hot toast. From the moral height of a cigarette she will pity hot toast.

Far from scheming to get the lady into a lunatic asylum, her hosts were extraordinarily sympathetic, and even when they were by themselves the worst thing they said was :

'Poor thing ! She's rather fussy about cigarettes.'

II

No one, I think, will assert that I have overdrawn the picture of a person victimised by a delusion and yet not inhabiting a lunatic asylum. Every one will be able out of his own experience of the world to match my example with examples of his own. And indeed there are few of us who are not familiar with at least one example immensely worse

THE COMPLETE FUSSER

than the lady who staked her daily existence on getting an Egyptian cigarette in her bath. Few of us have not met the gentleman who can only be described as ' the complete fusser.' This gentleman has slowly convinced himself that the proper fulfilment of his destiny depends alsolutely upon about ten thousand different things. All things of course have their importance, but this gentleman attaches a supreme and quite fatal importance to all the ten thousand things. He begins to be fussy on waking up, and he stops being fussy when he goes to sleep. He may not smoke a cigarette in his bath, but he will probably keep a thermometer in his bath because he is convinced that there is a 'right' temperature for the bath-water, and that any other temperature would impair his efficiency. He may detest smoking, in which case he will probably have rigid ideas about the precise sort of woven stuff he must wear next to his skin. He may be almost any kind of character, and yet be fussy. He may be so tidy that he cannot exist in a room, either in his own house or in anybody else's, until he has been round the walls and made all the pictures exactly horizontal. He may be so untidy that if his wife privily tidies his desk he is put off work for the rest of the day. He may be so fond of open air that he can only sleep with his head out of a window, or so afraid of open air that a draught deranges all his activities for a fortnight. He may be so regular that he kisses his wife by the clock, or so irregular that he is never conscious of appetite until a meal has been going cold for half an hour. And so on endlessly.

But whatever he does and thinks he does and thinks under the conviction that if he did and thought otherwise the consequences would be disastrous to himself if not to others. Whereas the truth is that to change all his

THE COMPLETE FUSSER

habits from morn to eve would result in great benefit to him. He spends his days attaching vast quantities of importance to a vast number of things. Whereas the truth is, that scarcely any of the said things are important in more than the slightest degree. He is the victim of not one delusion but of hundreds of delusions, and especially the grand delusion that the world is ready to come to an end on the most trifling provocation.

But there is no hope of him being sent to join the poached egg in the lunatic asylum. His friends are content to say of him:

'He's rather a particular man.'

True, his enemies scorn and objurgate him, and proclaim him pernicious to society. You naturally are his enemy, and you scorn him. But you should beware how you scorn him, because you may unconsciously be on the way to becoming a complete fusser yourself. All of us—or at any rate ninety-nine out of every hundred of us—have within us the insidious microbe of fussiness.

III

The way to becoming a complete fusser is obscure at the start of it. To determine the predisposing causes to fussiness would necessitate volumes of research into the secrets of individuality and the origins of character—and would assuredly lead to no practical result, because these creative mysteries lie beyond our influence—at any rate for the present. A man is born with or without the instinct to fuss—that must suffice for us.

Nevertheless the real instinct to fuss ought not to be confused with perfectly normal impulses which may superficially resemble it. Thus it is often assumed that domestic servants as a class are fussy, especially about their food. I can see no reason why domestic

THE COMPLETE FUSSER 95

servants as a class should be fussy, and I do not believe they are. What is mistaken for fussiness in them is merely the universal human prejudice against anything to which one is not accustomed. Labouring people are, unfortunately for themselves, used to a narrow diet. A hundred comestibles which to their alleged superiors may seem quite commonplace are fearsomely strange to labouring people. A rural girl goes to serve in a large house ; she is offered excellent fish, and she refuses it ; she 'can't fancy it.' Whereupon the mistress exclaims upon the astounding fussiness of the poor! The explanation of the affair is simply that the rural girl has never had opportunity to regard fish as an article of diet.

Similar phenomena may be observed in children of even the superior unfussy classes. And, for another instance, gardeners will grow the most superb asparagus who would not dream of eating it, and could scarcely bring themselves to eat it. For them asparagus is not a luxury, but something unnatural in the mouth, like snails or the hind-legs of frogs. Snails and the hind-legs of frogs are luxuries in various parts of the world; the Anglo-Saxon maid-scorning mistress would certainly recoil from them if they were put on her plate, and in so doing she would not lay herself open to a charge of fussiness. Yet in recoiling from them she would be behaving exactly like the rural maid whom she scorns.

Nor must fussiness be confused with certain profound and incurable antipathies, such as the strong repulsion of some individuals for cats, apples, horses, etc.

The real instinct to fuss can always be distinguished from the other thing by this—the real instinct to fuss is progressive. If it is not checked with extreme firmness it

THE COMPLETE FUSSER 97

goes steadily on its way. And though the start of the way to becoming a complete fusser may be obscure, the later portions of the journey are not so obscure. Pride, if not conceit, presides over them, and is always pushing forward the traveller from one abnormality to the next. Thus a man discloses a dislike to black clothes. His aunt dies at a great distance and leaves him some money. His wife asks him : ' Shall you wear black ? ' He answers with somewhat pained dignity : ' Darling, you know I never wear black.' He is now known to himself and to his wife as the man who will not wear black. Then his father dies, in the same town where the son lives ; the objector to black will have to attend the funeral. After a little conversation with him the wife says to friends : ' You know Edward objects to black. He does really. He *never* wears it, and I 'm afraid he won't wear it even for his father's funeral.'

Henceforth Edward is known not merely to himself and his wife but to the whole town as the man who won't wear black. It is a distinction. He is proud of it. His wife is rather impressed by the sturdiness of his resolution. He has suffered a little for his objection to black. His reputation is made. An anti-black clause inserts itself into his religion. Pride develops into conceit. Success and renown encourage the instinct to fuss, and soon he has grown fussy about something else. And thus does the fellow reach his goal of being a complete fusser.

IV

There is no cure for the complete fusser. You might think that some tremendous disaster—such as marrying a shrew who hated fussing, or being cast on a desert island, or being imprisoned—would cure him. But it would not. It would only cause a change in

THE COMPLETE FUSSER 99

the symptoms; for every human environment whatsoever gives occasion for fussiness to the complete fusser. Even in the army, even in the lowest and most order-ridden grades of the army, the complete fusser contrives to flourish. And he is incurable because he is unconscious of being fussy. What the world regards as fussiness he regards as wisdom essential to a reasonable existence. He sincerely looks down upon the rest of mankind. Spiritual pride puts him into the category of the hopeless case—along with the alcoholic drunkard, the genuine kleptomaniac, and other specimens whom he would chillingly despise.

Apparently the sole use of the complete fusser is to serve as a terrible warning to those who are on the way to becoming complete fussers themselves—a terrible warning to pull up.

That fussiness in its earlier stages can be

cured is certain. But the cure is very drastic in nature. There are lucid moments in the life of the as yet incomplete fusser when he suspects his malady, when he guiltily says to himself: 'I know I am peculiar, but—' Such a moment must be seized, and immediate action taken. (The 'but' must be choked. The 'but' may be full of wisdom, but it must be choked; the 'but' is fatal.) If the fusser is anti-black let him proceed to the shopping quarter at once. Let him not order a suit-to-measure of black. Let him buy a ready-made suit. Let him put it on in the store or shop, and let him have the other suit sent home. Let him then walk about the town in black. . . . He is saved! No less thorough procedure will save him.

And similarly for all other varieties of fussiness.

THE MEANING OF FROCKS

THE MEANING OF FROCKS

I

BEING a man, I know that on the subject of women's fashions men still talk a vast amount of nonsense, partly sincere and partly insincere—especially when there are no women present. The fact is that the whole subject is deeply misunderstood, and the great majority of people, both men and women, live and dress and die without getting anywhere near the truth of it.

Men try to explain the feminine cult of clothes by asserting that women as a sex are vain. It is a profound truth that women as a sex are vain. It is also a profound truth that men as a sex are vain. Have you ever been with a man into a hosier's shop? If you are a woman you certainly have not, because, though a woman is often glad to be accompanied by a man when she is choosing her adornments, a man will not allow a woman to watch him at the same work. Fashionable dressmakers are delighted to welcome the accompanying man. But at the sight of a woman in his establishment the fashionable hosier would begin to fear for the safety of the commonwealth. Even if you are a man you probably have not been with another man into a hosier's shop. Men prefer to do these deeds quite alone ; they shun even their own sex ; the shopman does not count. Why this secrecy ? The answer is clear. Men are ashamed of themselves on such occasions because on such occasions their real vanity is exposed. Tailors, hosiers, and hatters are a loyal clan ; but it must be admitted that they all have a strange look on their faces. That look is due to the revelations of male vanity which they carry locked eternally in their breasts. To these purveyors men give

THE MEANING OF FROCKS

themselves away and are shameless before them. The ordinary man well knows that he is vain. Besides, you can see him surreptitiously glancing at himself in shop windows any day. And in some American periodicals there are positively more advertisements of men's finery than of women's.

Again, men try to explain the feminine cult of clothes by asserting that women are like sheep and must follow one another. What one does all must do. This argument is more than insincere; it is impudent. For women show much wider originality and variations of attire among themselves than men do among themselves. Half a dozen average well-dressed women will be as different one from another as half a dozen flowers of different species; you could distinguish between them half a mile off. But half a dozen well-dressed men would be indistinguishably alike if you decapitated them. It is notorious that men are the slaves of fashion.

If a new shade of cravat or sock comes out, the city will be painted with that shade in less than a week. One year every handkerchief is worn in the sleeve. Another year it will be shocking to wear a handkerchief in the sleeve, because the only proper place for wearing a handkerchief is in a pocket over the heart. At the slightest change in the fashionable diameter of the leg of a pair of trousers every man with adequate cash or credit will rush privily to his tailor's, and in sixty hours a parcel will arrive at that man's home marked : 'Very urgent. Deliver at once.'

Men have a perfect passion for being exactly like other men—not merely in clothes, but in everything. So much so that they cannot bear to think that there are men unlike themselves. Thus men will form clubs of which all the members are alike in some important point, so that while they are in the club they will live under the beautiful illusion of universal resemblance. They loathe opinions which are unfashionable, or unfashionable in their particular set and environment; they will not even read about such opinions if they can help it; they are ready to imprison or kill (and often actually have imprisoned or killed) the holders of such opinions, solely because they are not in the fashion. And could a man with a bag-wig walk down the Strand or Fifth Avenue without having it knocked off or being arrested for obstruction? He could not. Nevertheless a bag-wig is less preposterous than a silk hat.

Yet again, men try to explain the feminine cult of clothes by asserting that women as a sex really enjoy the huge task of dressing, and really enjoy spending money for the sake of spending money, and have no brains above personal embellishment. All these arguments are patently ridiculous. To very many well-dressed women the task of dressing is naught but a tedious and heavy burden. As for brains, it frequently occurs that the women with the most intelligence (intelligence far surpassing that of the average man) are the most *chic*. In regard to the enjoyment of mere spending, the charge is true. It is, however, equally true of men. I could refer to tailors, hosiers, and hatters, but I will not. Take, for a change, two dining parties at a restaurant, one consisting of three men and three women, the other consisting of six men. The bill of the six men will be the heavier. As a sex men, in the French phrase, 'refuse themselves nothing.' And their felicity in spending for the sake of spending is touchingly boyish.

Whatever may be the explanation of the subjection of women to costly fashion, we are now, at any rate, in a position to say what the explanation is *not*. It is not that women are specially vain. It is not that women are specially like sheep. It is not that they lack intelligence. It is not that they enjoy the tyranny. And it is not that they are spendthrift. If the explanation lay in any of these directions men would read fashion papers, go to sales, and change their suits four times a day.

II

You will say :

'Women adorn themselves in order to be attractive to the other sex.'

This is true, but only to a limited extent. And men also adorn themselves in order to be attractive to the other sex. Moreover, a woman who has found the man of her desire, and is utterly satisfied therewith, will still go on adorning herself, even though the man in question has made it quite clear that she would attract him just as strongly in a sack as in a Poiret gown. Further, some fashions do not attract ; they excite ridicule rather than admiration ; yet they are persisted in. And women of the classes who do not and cannot cultivate fashionableness succeed at least as well as the other woman in attracting men, even when these men by reason of laborious lives have almost no leisure for dalliance. The truth is that the competition among women for men is chiefly a legend—not wholly. There are more women than men, but not many more. Women want marriage more than men want marriage, but not much more. Competition is by no means so fierce that women have to perform prodigies of self-ornamentation in order to inveigle a fellow-creature so simple that he worries about the tint of his own necktie and socks; and the idea of such a phenomenon is derogatory to women. After all, nature has the business of sex-attraction in hand, and she is not dependent on fashions. Long before fashions had been evolved she managed it precisely as well as she manages it to-day. She relies, not upon textile stuffs, but upon the stuff that dreams are made on; namely, glances, gestures, actions, and speech.

The authentic major explanation of the

THE MEANING OF FROCKS

expensive fashionableness of women must be sought in another direction. As usual, men are at the bottom of the affair. When woman gloriously dresses herself up to go out, she does so in order to prove to the world something which man wants to be proved to the world. In old days the two attributes which man held in the highest esteem were wealth and idleness. To be poor was shameful, and to work for a living was shameful. Man, therefore, had to demonstrate publicly that he was neither needy nor industrious. One of the best methods of demonstration was costume, and the costume of the successful man in those days was very expensive, and so gorgeous and delicate as to make toil impossible for him.

The time came when man ceased to be proud of his own idleness, and his costume altered accordingly. Then the duty of demonstrating wealth and idleness by means of costume fell on woman. Man could not do the demonstration on his own person—he was too busy—and hence he employed the lady to be expensive on his behalf. Such was her function, and still is her function. The Rue de la Paix is based firmly on the distant past. Assuredly long years will elapse before feminine costume ceases to be used as a demonstration that man possesses the attributes that are most admired. Estates demonstrate the possession of those attributes; bonds demonstrate the possession of those attributes. But estates are a fixture, and bonds are kept in a safe. Costume walks about; your wife can take it to the seaside with her; the world cannot help noticing it; and it has the further advantage of ministering to the senses.

The proofs of the substantial correctness of this explanation of women's dress are innumerable. Perhaps the principal proof is that the very man who grumbles at fashionableness in women would be the first to com-

THE MEANING OF FROCKS

plain if his wife started to ignore fashion and to dress merely for comfort, utility, and charm. No man objects to the inexpensiveness of his wife's clothes, but every man objects to them looking inexpensive. The advertised lure of a blouse marked one pound at a sale is that it has the air of a blouse costing two pounds. Suppose a rich man sees a delightful typewriting young woman walking down the street, falls in love with her, and marries her. Now, although the clothes in which he saw her suited her admirably in every way, and although she has simple tastes, and more elaborate clothes do not suit her so well, the first thing she has to do on marriage is to alter her style of dress for a more expensive style. Otherwise the man will say: 'I don't want my wife to look like a clerk.' In other words: 'I insist on my wife demonstrating to the universe that I possess wealth and can afford to keep her idle on my behalf.' Even in small provincial towns where personal adornment is theoretically discouraged, and where people preach the entirely false maxim that externals don't matter—even there the theory holds good. The middle-class wife will have her sealskin coat before she has her automobile. Fur coats are detestable garments to walk in, but real sealskin is a symbol which cannot be denied.

And it is as important that that costume should prove idleness as that it should prove wealth. Hence the fragility of extremely fashionable costumes, and their unpracticalness. The fashionable costume must be of such a nature that the least touch of the workaday world will ruin it; and it must go beyond this—it must be of such a nature that the wearer is actually prevented by it from her full and proper activity. An unconsidered movement would rip it to pieces. Rich Chinese males till recently kept their finger-nails so long that it was impossible

THE MEANING OF FROCKS

for them to use their hands, and they maimed females so that they could not walk. Both sexes were thus rendered helpless, and the ability to be futile was proved like a problem of Euclid. We laugh at that. Crinolines were admirably designed to hinder honest work. And we laugh at crinolines too. But we still have the corset, though the corset is not the homicidal contrivance it once was. And we have the high-heeled shoe, higher than ever. You say: 'But women have high heels to increase their apparent height.' Not a bit! All women whose business it is to demonstrate idleness to the universe wear high heels, because high heels are a clear presumption that the wearer is not obliged really to exert herself. If a woman with a rich husband is so inordinately tall that she is ashamed of her height, she will wear high heels to prove that her husband is rich. And, not to be outdone, the delightful typewriting girl walking down the street at 8.30 A.M. will also wear high heels—and each hurried step she takes is a miracle of balance, pluck, and endurance. Life is marvellous.

III

You will say :

'Life may be marvellous, but these revelations about human motives are terrible, and they depress us.'

They ought not to depress you. The saving quality about human motives is that they are so human, and therefore so forgivable. And, be it remembered, I have not asserted that the demonstration of wealth and leisure is the sole explanation of fashionableness. I have already referred to the desire to be attractive ; and to this must be added the sense of beauty, which is nearly allied to it. The woman who bedecks herself is actuated by all three motives—the motive of ostentation (to satisfy primarily the man), the motive to attract, and the motive to satisfy the sense of beauty.

As regards the last, it may be said that the

THE MEANING OF FROCKS

sense of beauty does not regularly improve in mankind, like, for instance, the sense of justice. No feminine raiment has ever equalled the classic Greek, which was not costly. But then the Greeks were not worried by too much wealth. And the Greek dress would be highly inconvenient without the Greek daily life, and especially without the Greek climate. And I doubt if nowadays we should care greatly for the Greek life. Still, the sense of beauty does emphatically exist among us, and the desire of women to be attractive is quite as powerful as it was in the time of Aspasia. These two motives are constantly, and often victoriously, fighting against the motive of ostentation, and it is probably the interplay of the three motives that produces the continual confusing and expensive changes of fashion, as has been well argued by Professor Franklin Henry Giddings, one of the most brilliant social philosophers in the United States.

' But all this must be altered ! ' the ardent

among you will cry out. ' In future women must dress solely to be attractive and to satisfy the sense of beauty.'

Well, they just won't. Men will never allow it, and women themselves would never agree to it. Costume will always be more than costume; costume is so handy and effective as a symbol of something else; and that something else will always be—success. When wealth ceases to be the standard of success, then costume will cease to be employed as a proof of wealth, and not before. Meanwhile, we must admit that, if the possession of wealth has to be proved to the world, it could not be proved in a more charming and less offensive way than in the costumes of women. The spectacle of a stylish dress stylishly worn is extremely agreeable. The spectacle of a room full of stylish dresses stylishly worn is thrilling. He among you who has never been to a ball should go to one and try the experience for himself.

Leisure, the ability to be idle and useless,

THE MEANING OF FROCKS

is still to a certain extent a standard of success in life, but not anything like so much as in the past. People are gradually perceiving that to be idle and useless is vicious. Hence the unpracticalness of women's costumes will gradually decrease. Beyond question high heels, for example, will vanish from our pavements and from our drawing-rooms. I even have hope that women will one day wear dresses which they can put on and fasten unaided without the help of one, two, or three assistants. But such changes will arrive slowly. You cannot hurry nature. It is a great truth that the present is firmly rooted in the past. It refuses to be pulled up by the roots. Futile to announce that you will in future be guided by nothing but common sense! Whose common sense? Common sense is a purely relative thing. The common sense of the past often seems silly to us, and the common sense of the present will often seem silly to the future. The progress of mankind is an extraordinarily complex business. It cannot be settled in a phrase. Nothing in it is simple; nothing in it is unrelated to the rest. Everything in it has a reason which will appeal to true intelligence. And men should bear this in mind when they talk lightly and scornfully (and foolishly) about women's fashions.

To conclude, let me utter one word about the secret fear that lies always at the back of most men's minds—the fear that such-and-such a change in the habits of women will destroy their femininity. This fear is groundless. Femininity — thank heaven !— is entirely indestructible. It will survive all progress and all revolutions of taste. And when the end comes on this cooling planet the last vestige of it will be there, fronting the last vestige of masculinity.

www.ingramcontent.com/pod-product-compliance
Lightning Source LLC
Chambersburg PA
CBHW032232080426
42735CB00008B/822